CASTING CROWNS
LIFESONG

ISBN 1-4234-1266-4

HAL•LEONARD®
CORPORATION
7777 W. BLUEMOUND RD. P.O. BOX 13819 MILWAUKEE, WI 53213

Visit Hal Leonard Online at
www.halleonard.com

LIFESONG

Words and Music by
MARK HALL

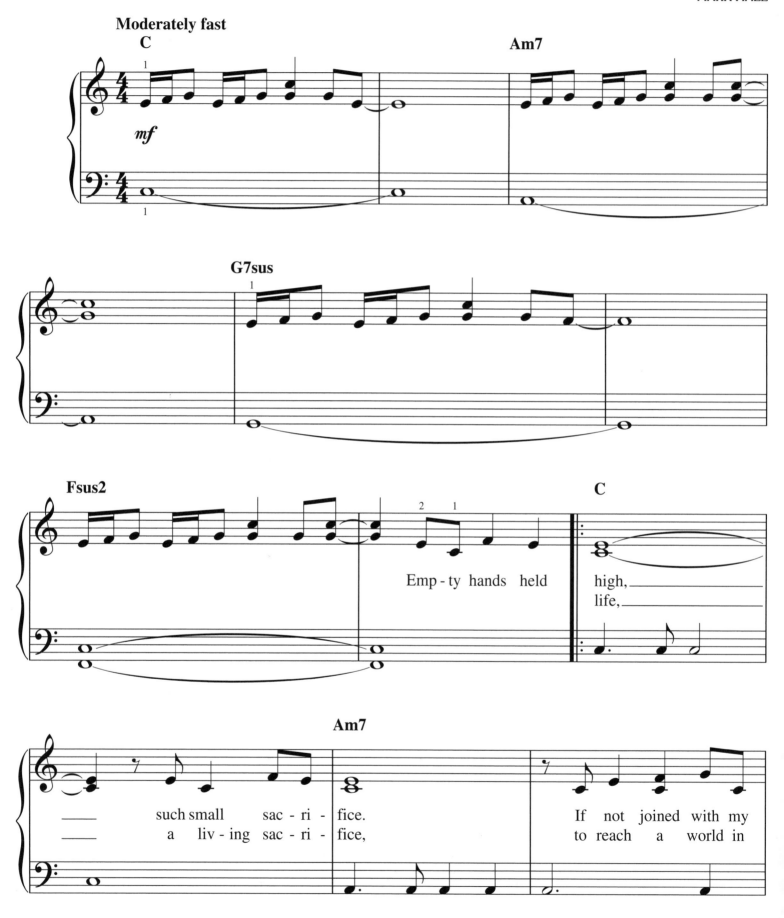

F   Dm7

life,   I sing in vain to - night.
need,   to be Your hands and feet.

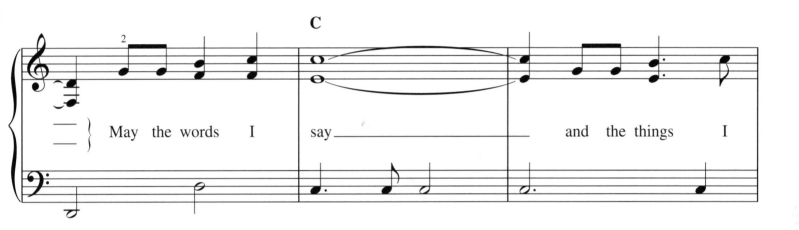

C

May the words I say   and the things I

Am7   Gsus

do   make my life - song sing,

F

bring a smile to You.   Let my

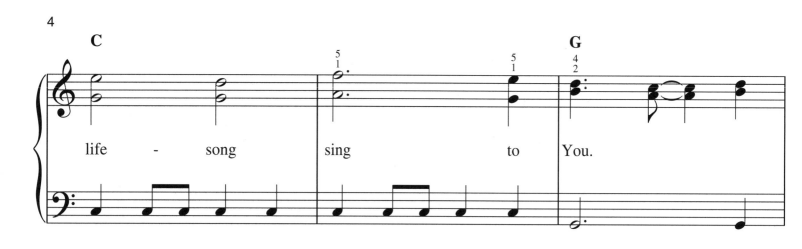

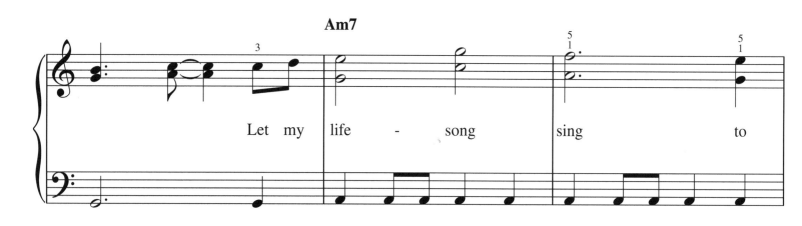

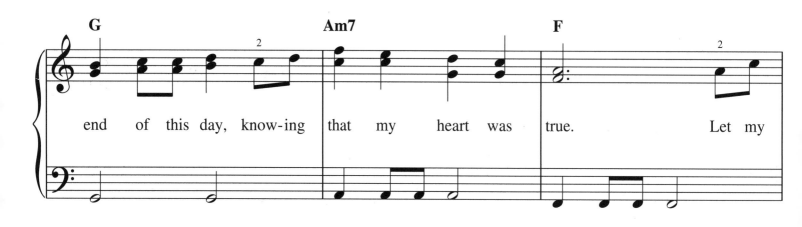

5

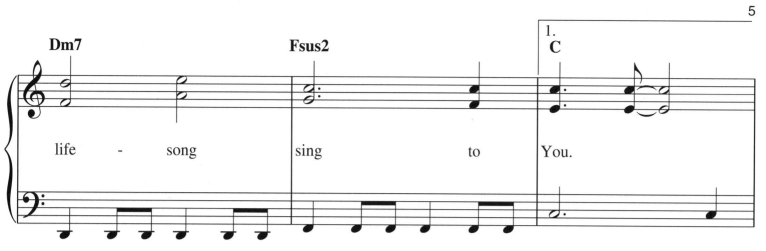

life - song sing to You.

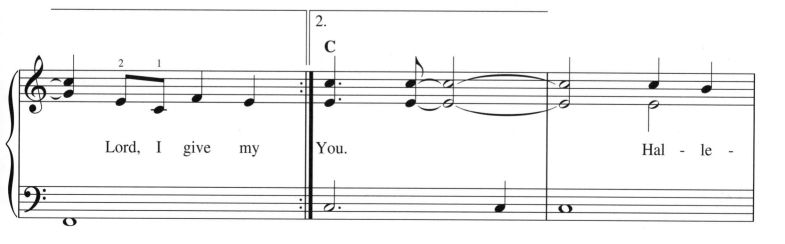

Lord, I give my You. Hal - le -

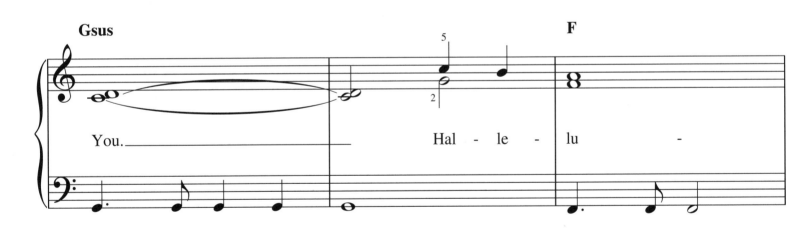

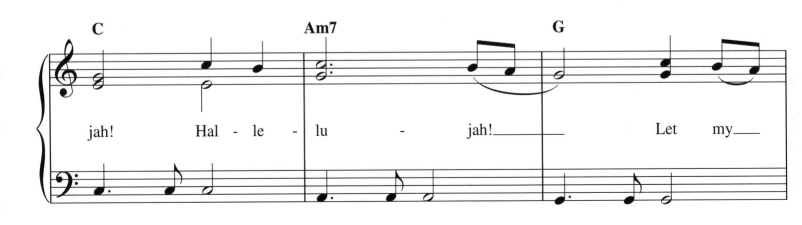

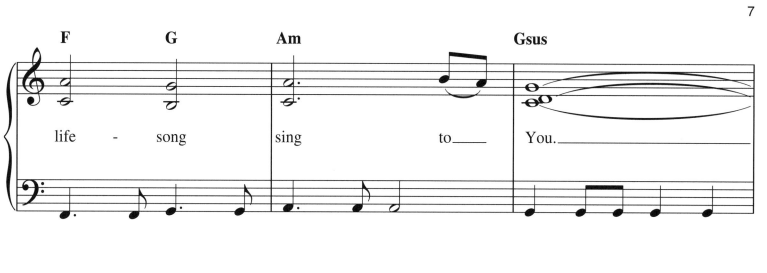

life - song   sing   to____   You._____

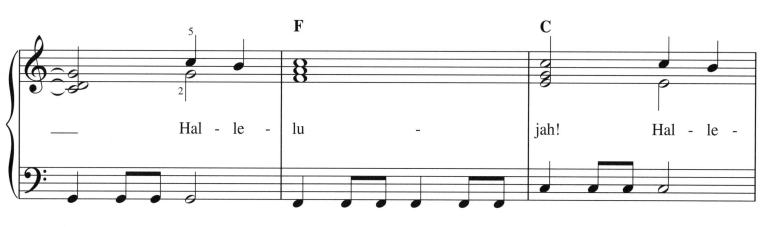

____ Hal - le - lu   -   jah!   Hal - le -

lu   -   jah!   Let my____   life - song

sing   to   You.   Let my

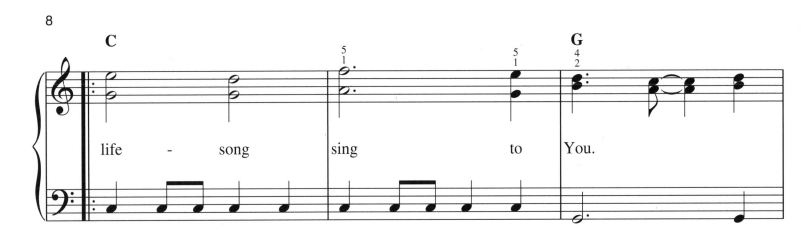

life - song   sing   to   You.

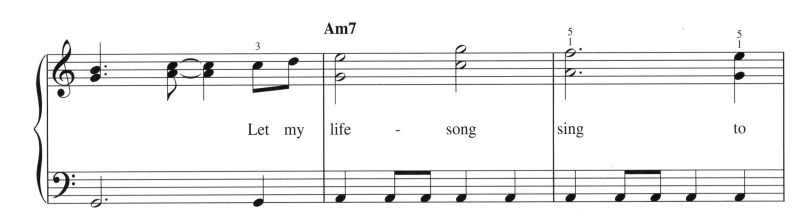

Let my   life - song   sing   to

You.   I want to   sign Your   name to the

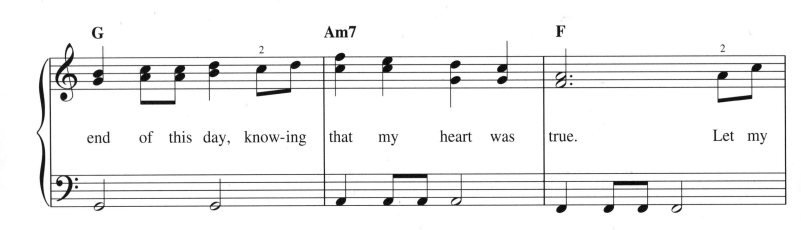

end   of this day, know-ing   that   my   heart was   true.   Let my

PRAISE YOU IN THIS STORM

Words and Music by MARK HALL
and BERNIE HERMS

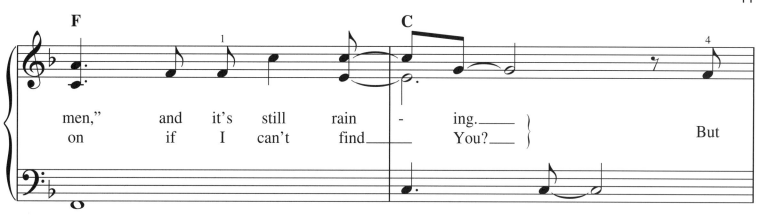

men," and it's still rain - ing.____
on if I can't find____ You?___ } But

as the thun - der rolls, I bare - ly hear You whis - per through the

rain, "I'm with you."_ And as Your mer - cy falls, I

raise my hands and praise the God who gives and takes a -

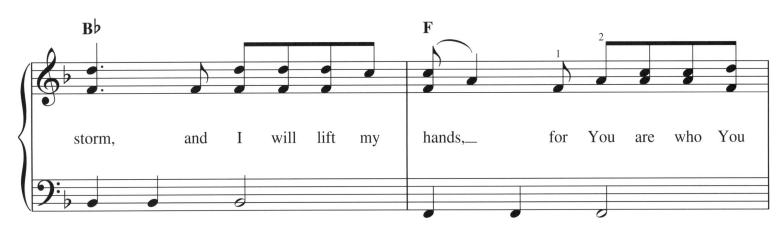

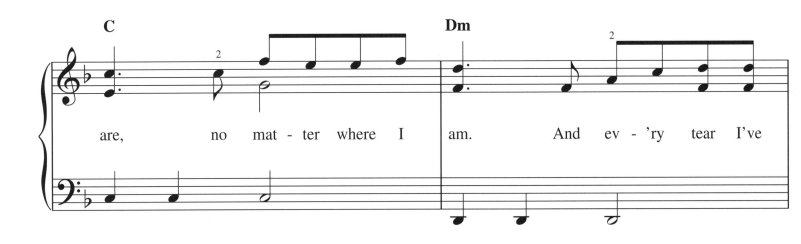

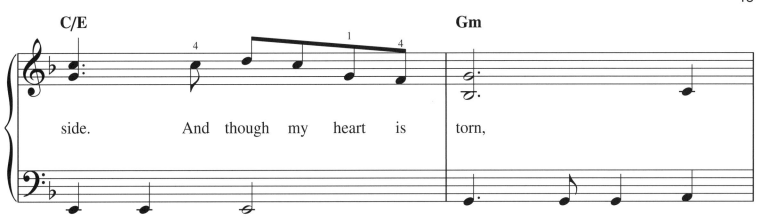

side.　　And though my heart is　torn,

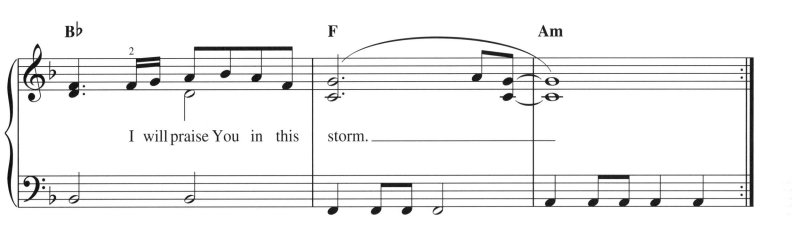

I will praise You in this　storm. _____

I lift my eyes un - to the hills.　Where does my help come　from?

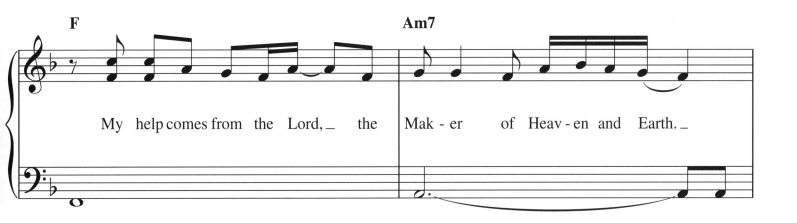

My help comes from the Lord, _ the　Mak - er　of Heav - en and Earth. _

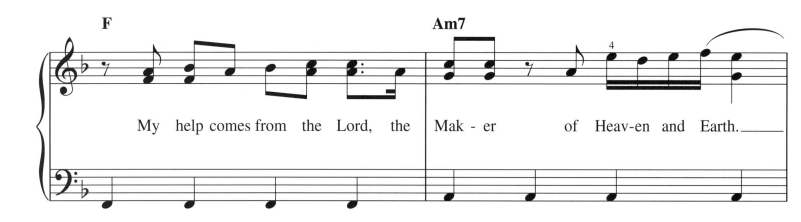

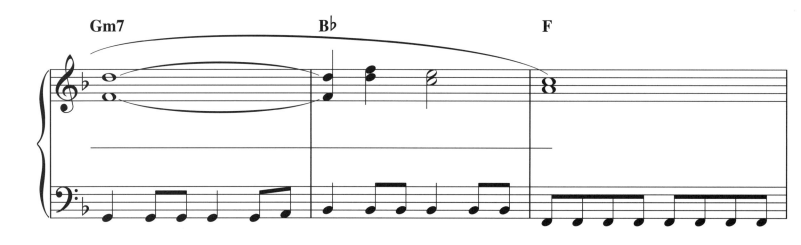

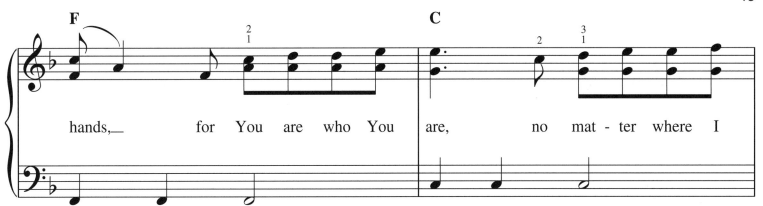

hands,___ for You are who You are, no mat-ter where I

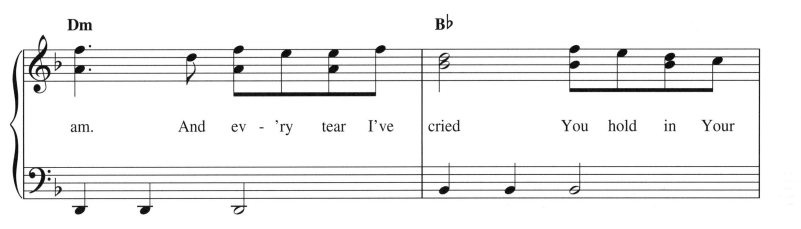

am. And ev-'ry tear I've cried You hold in Your

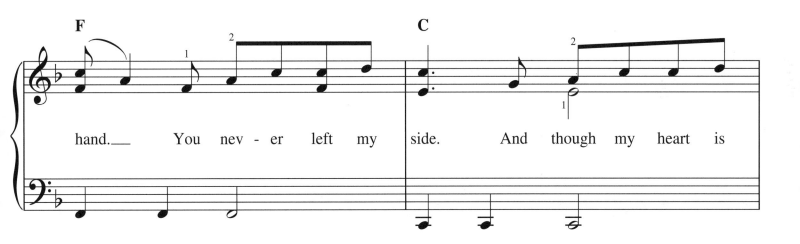

hand.___ You nev-er left my side. And though my heart is

torn,_____ I will praise You in this storm.___

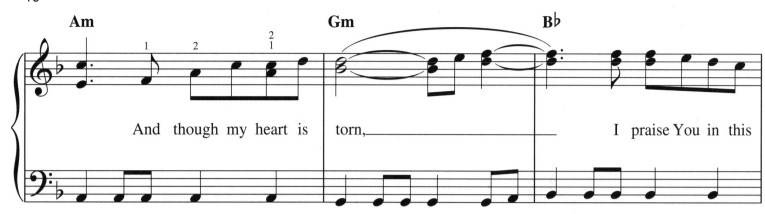

And though my heart is torn,_____ I praise You in this

storm.

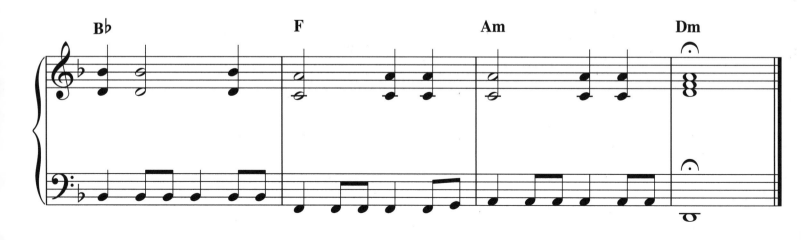

DOES ANYBODY HEAR HER

Words and Music by
MARK HALL

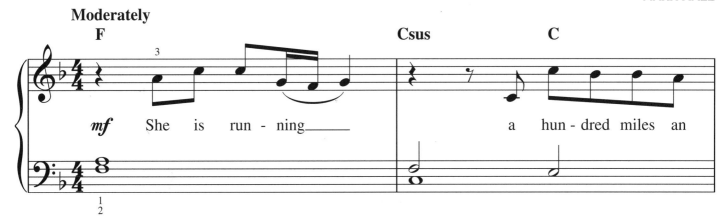

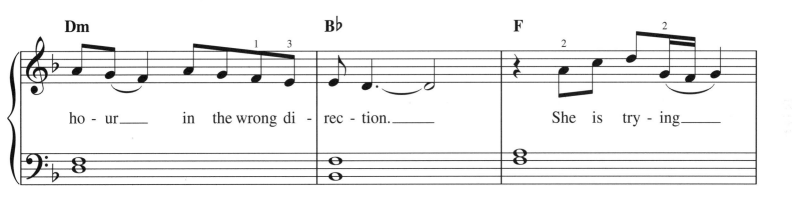

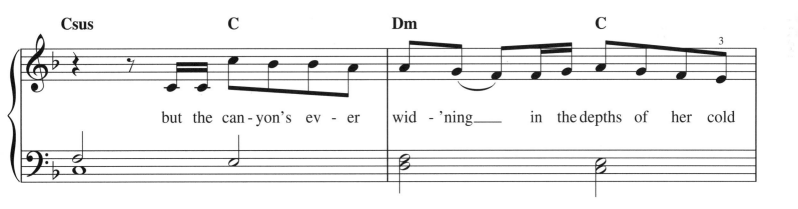

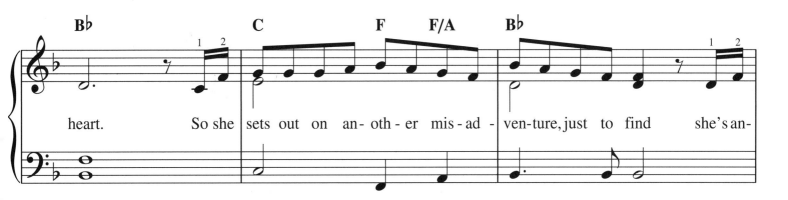

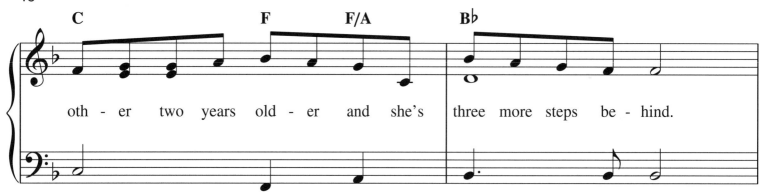

C   F   F/A   B♭

oth - er two years old - er and she's three more steps be - hind.

B♭(add2)   ℅ F

Does an - y - bod - y hear her? Can an - y - bod - y

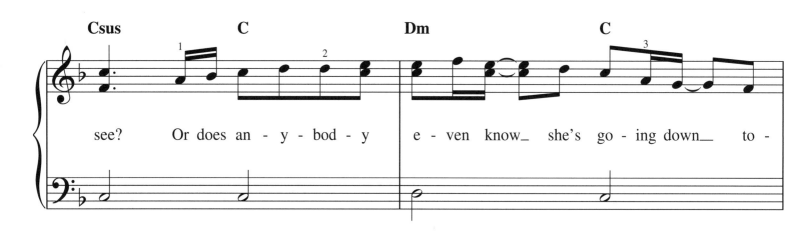

Csus   C   Dm   C

see? Or does an - y - bod - y e - ven know___ she's go - ing down___ to -

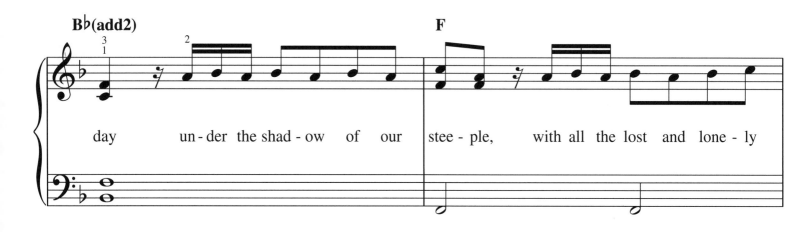

B♭(add2)   F

day un - der the shad - ow of our stee - ple, with all the lost and lone - ly

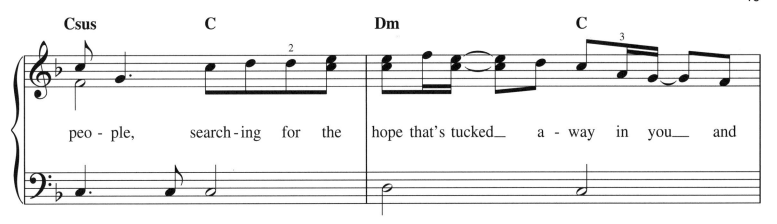

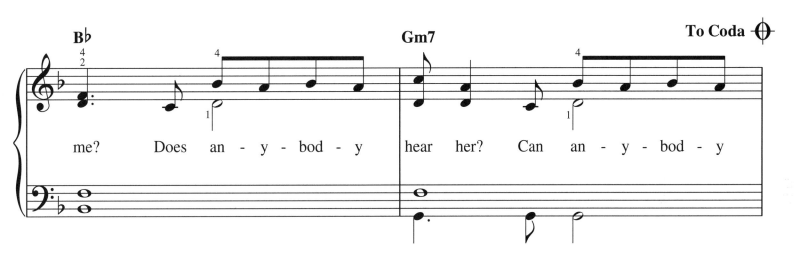

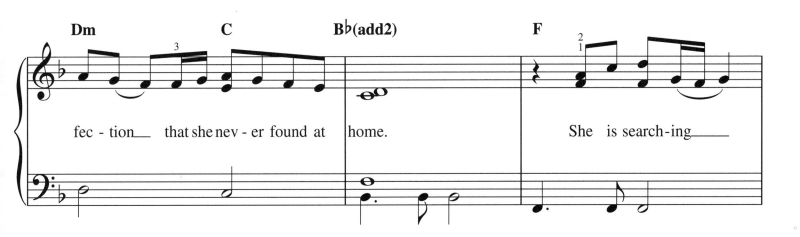

for a he-ro to ride in, to ride in and save the day. And

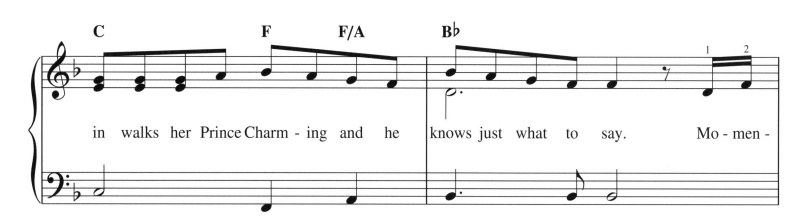

in walks her Prince Charm-ing and he knows just what to say. Mo-men-

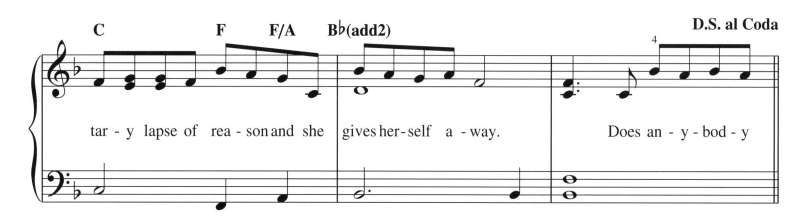

D.S. al Coda

tar-y lapse of rea-son and she gives her-self a-way. Does an-y-bod-y

CODA

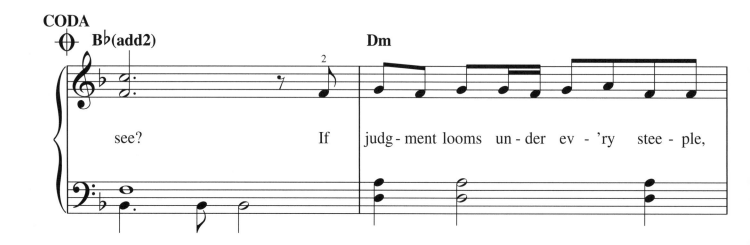

see? If judg-ment looms un-der ev-'ry stee-ple,

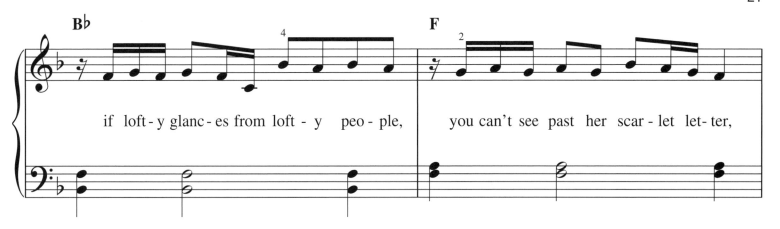

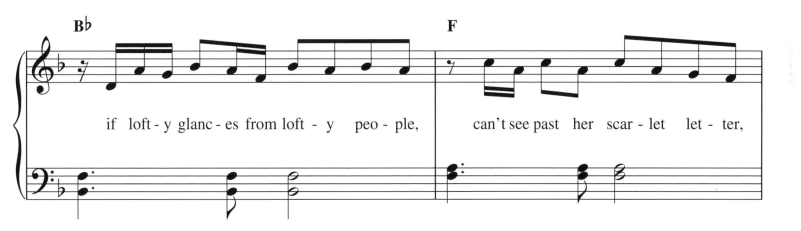

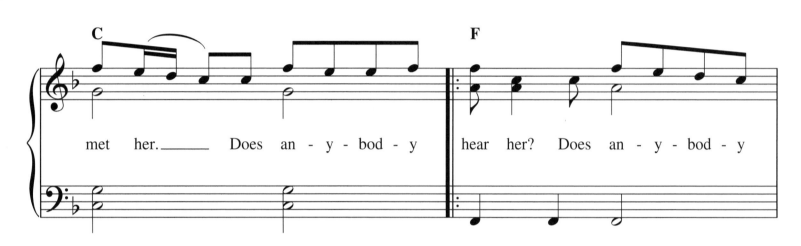

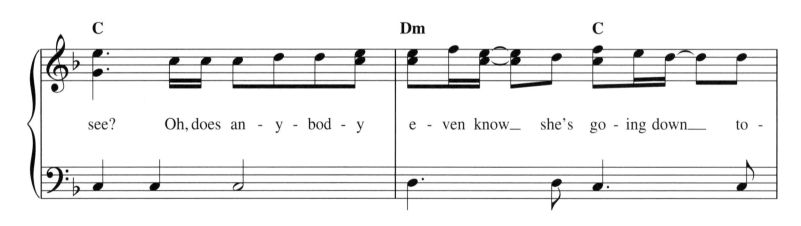

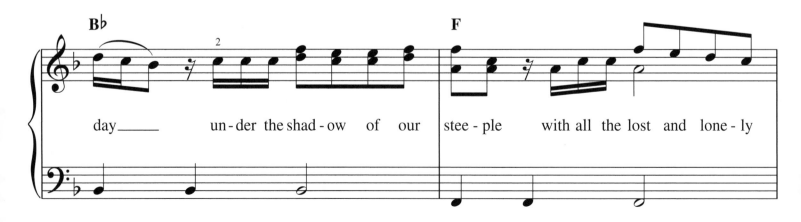

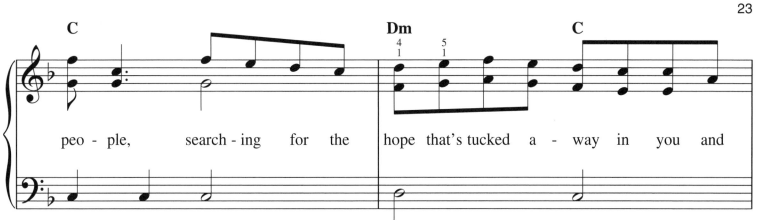

peo - ple, search - ing for the hope that's tucked a - way in you and

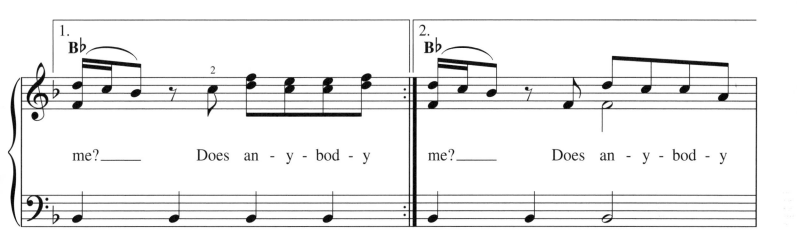

1.
me?_____ Does an - y - bod - y

2.
me?_____ Does an - y - bod - y

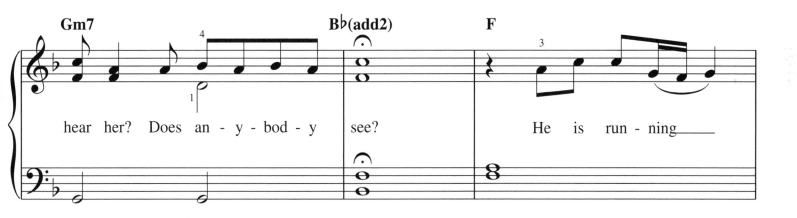

hear her? Does an - y - bod - y see? He is run - ning_____

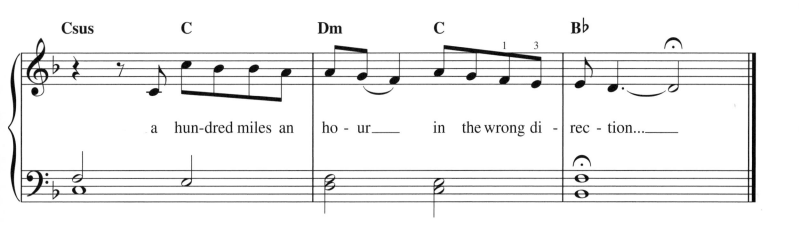

a hun-dred miles an ho - ur_____ in the wrong di - rec - tion..._____

STAINED GLASS MASQUERADE

Words and Music by MARK HALL
and NICHOLE NORDEMAN

Moderate Rock beat

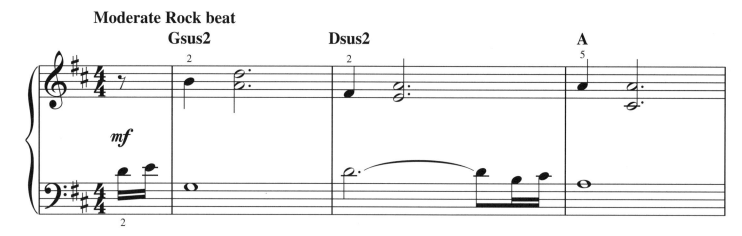

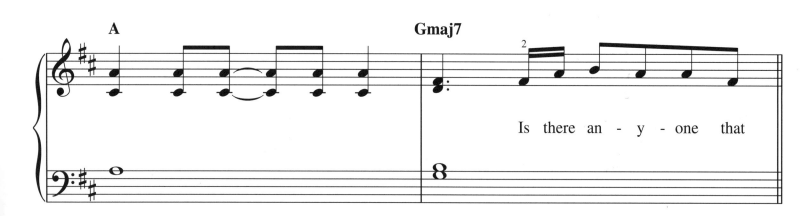

Is there an - y - one that

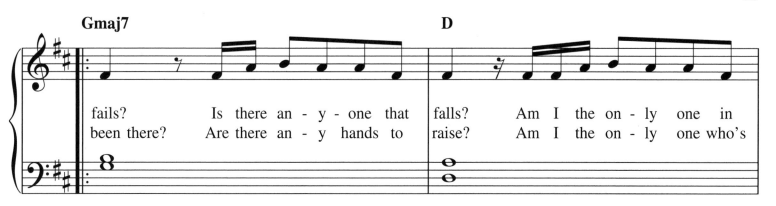

fails?   Is there an - y - one that | falls?   Am I the on - ly   one in
been there?   Are there an - y hands to | raise?   Am I the on - ly   one who's

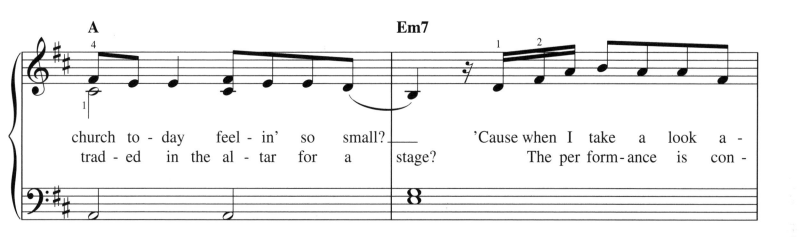

church to - day   feel - in' so   small? | 'Cause when I take   a   look a -
trad - ed   in the al - tar   for   a | stage?   The per form - ance is   con -

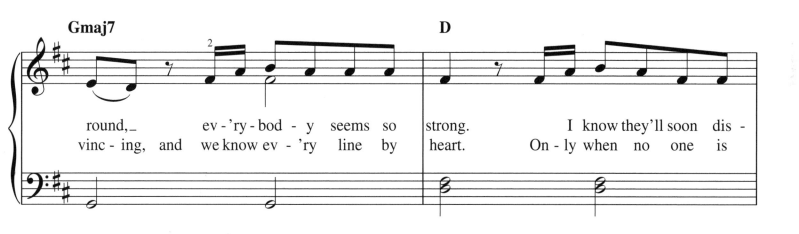

round,__   ev - 'ry - bod - y seems so | strong.   I know they'll soon dis -
vinc - ing, and we know ev - 'ry line by | heart.   On - ly when no one is

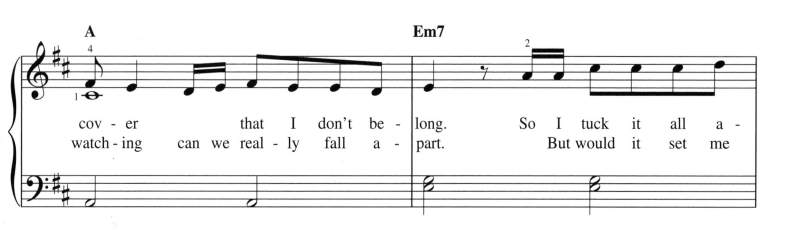

cov - er   that I don't be - | long.   So I tuck it all a -
watch - ing   can we real - ly fall a - | part.   But would it set me

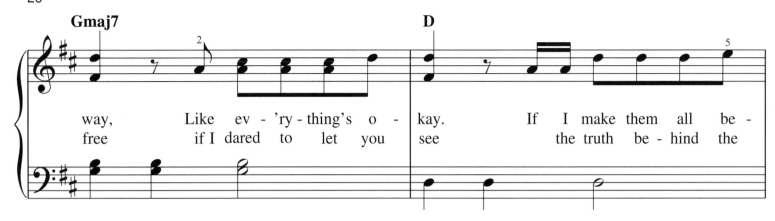

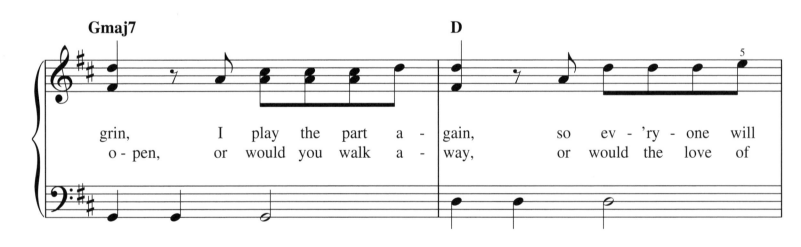

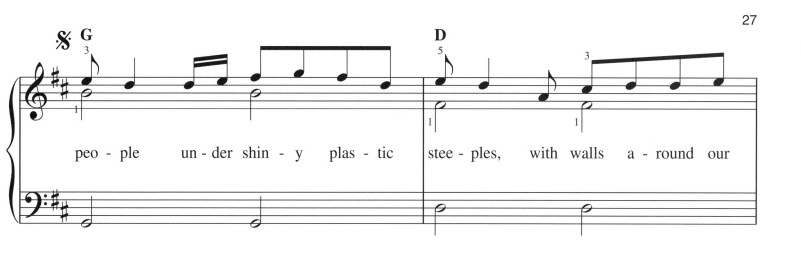

peo - ple   un - der shin - y   plas - tic   stee - ples,   with walls a - round our

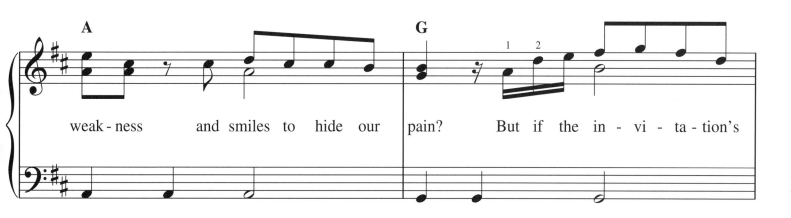

weak - ness   and smiles to hide our   pain?   But if the in - vi - ta - tion's

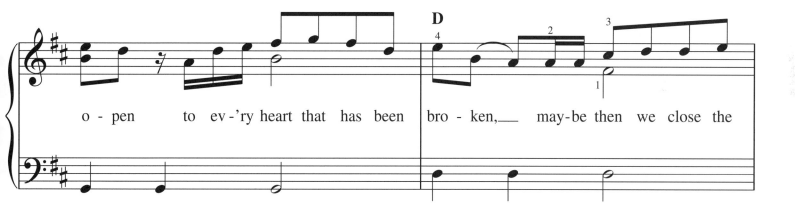

o - pen   to ev - 'ry heart that has been   bro - ken,___   may - be then we close the

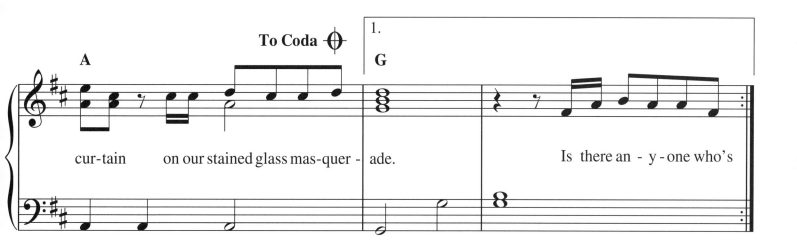

To Coda

1.

cur - tain   on our stained glass mas - quer - ade.   Is there an - y - one who's

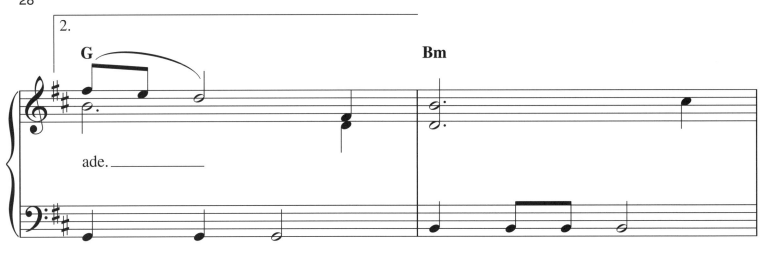

G **Bm**

ade. _____

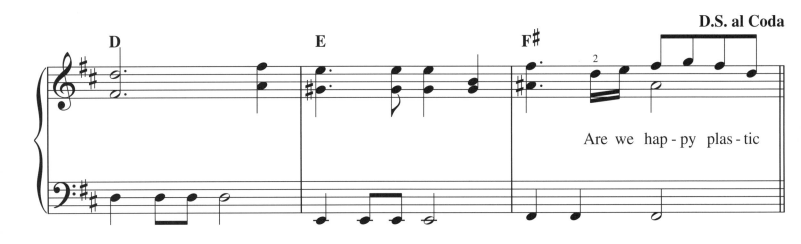

D **E** **F♯** **D.S. al Coda**

Are we hap - py plas - tic

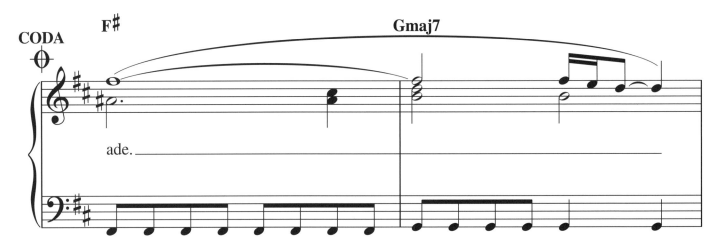

CODA **F♯** **Gmaj7**

ade. _____

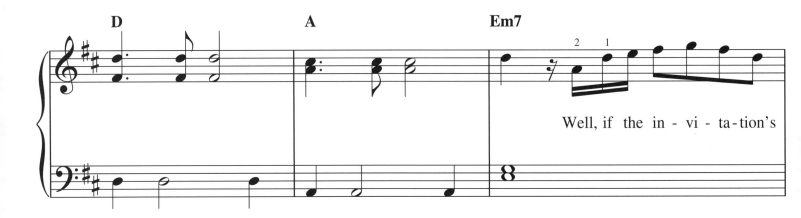

D **A** **Em7**

Well, if the in - vi - ta - tion's

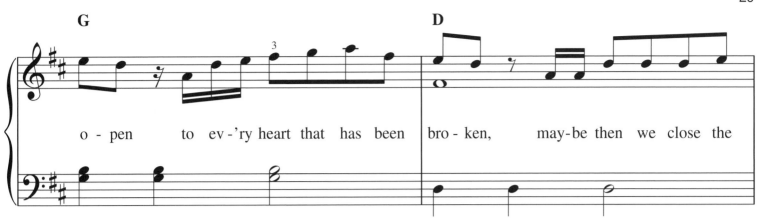

o - pen to ev-'ry heart that has been bro - ken, may-be then we close the

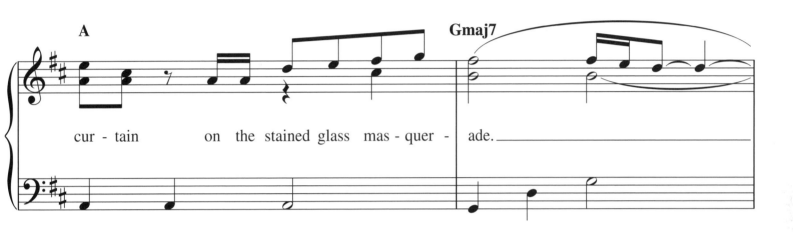

cur - tain on the stained glass mas - quer - ade._____

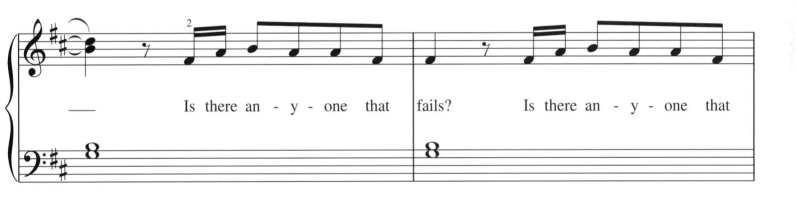

_____ Is there an - y - one that fails? Is there an - y - one that

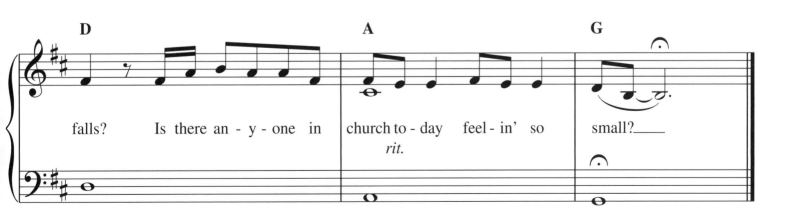

falls? Is there an - y - one in church to - day feel - in' so small?_____

rit.

LOVE THEM LIKE JESUS

Words and Music by MARK HALL
and BERNIE HERMS

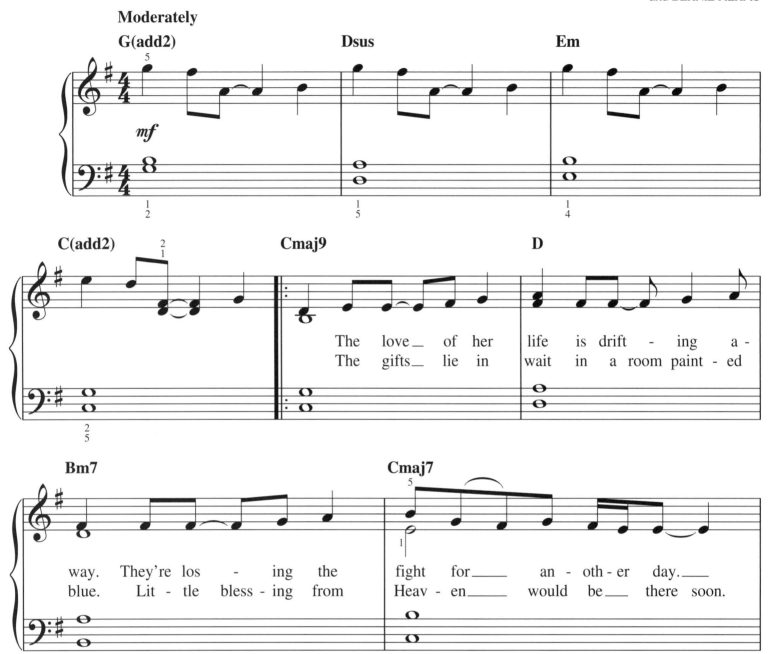

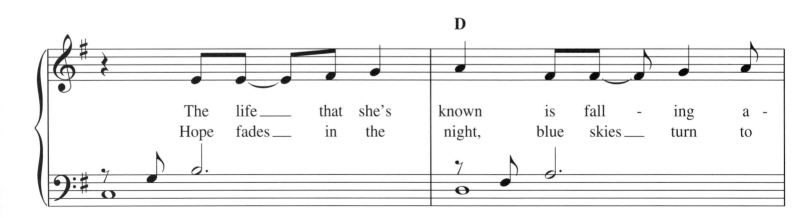

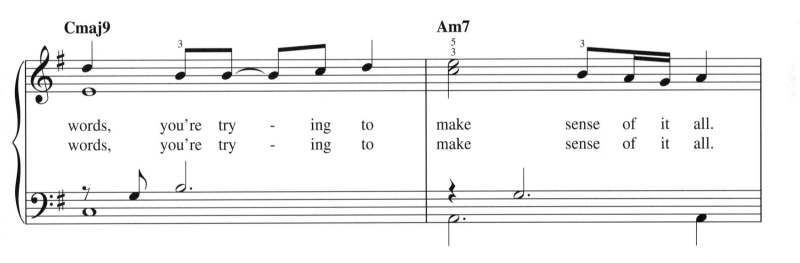

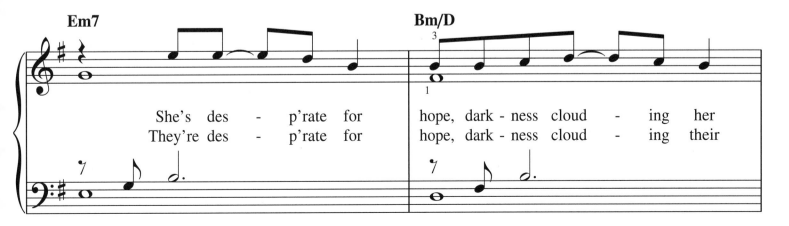

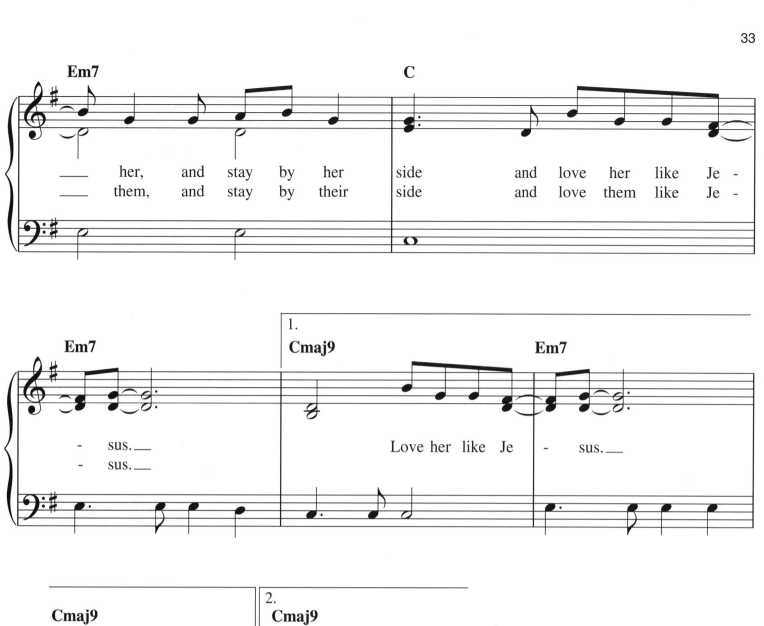

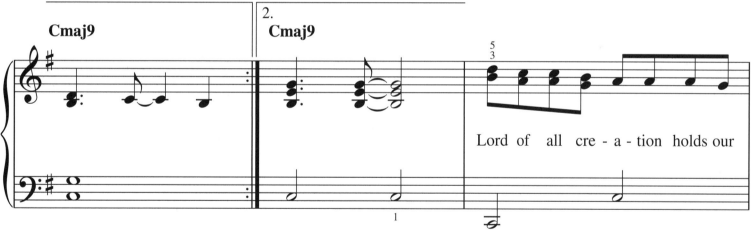

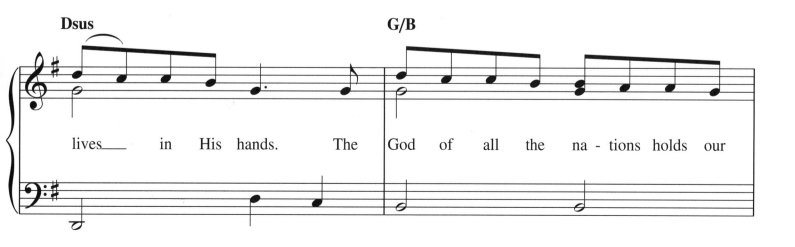

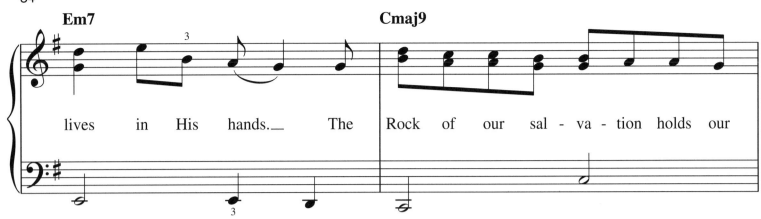

Em7 ... **Cmaj9**

lives in His hands.___ The Rock of our sal - va - tion holds our

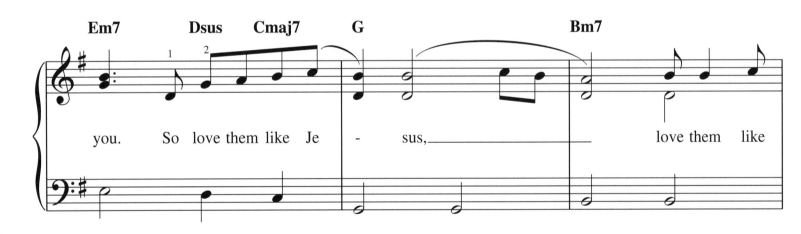

Dsus ... **G/B**

lives___ in His hands. He cares for them just as He cares for

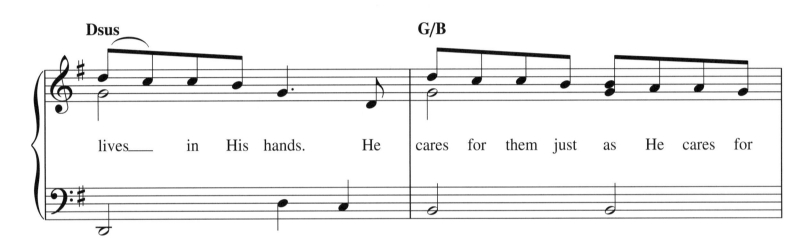

Em7 **Dsus** **Cmaj7** **G** ... **Bm7**

you. So love them like Je - sus,___ love them like

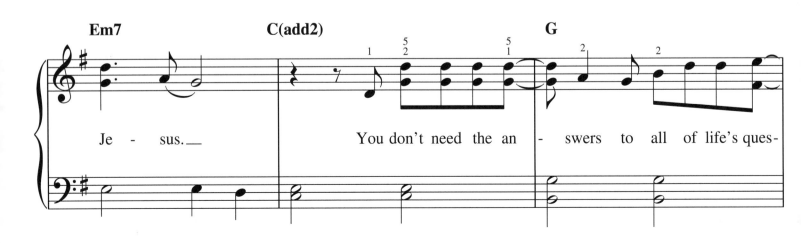

Em7 ... **C(add2)** ... **G**

Je - sus.___ You don't need the an - swers to all of life's ques-

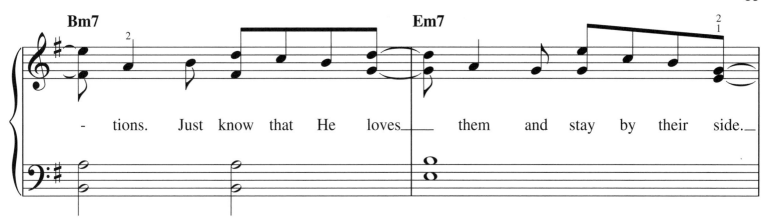

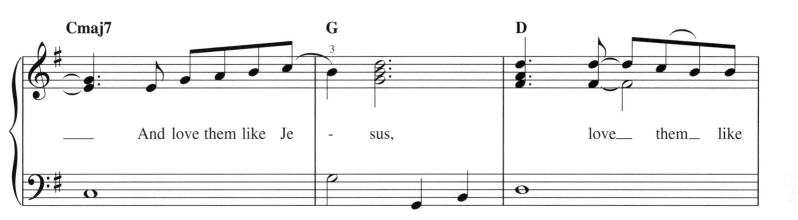

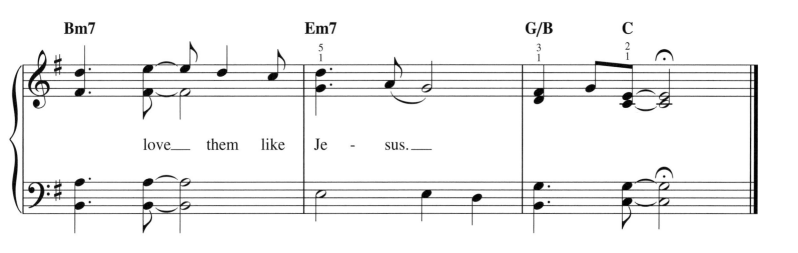

SET ME FREE

Words by MARK HALL
Music by MARK HALL and BERNIE HERMS

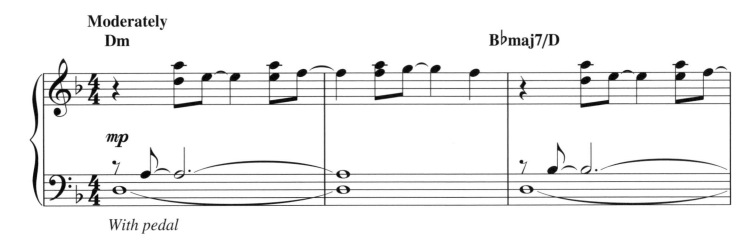

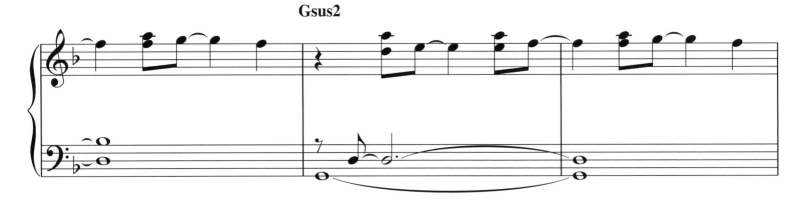

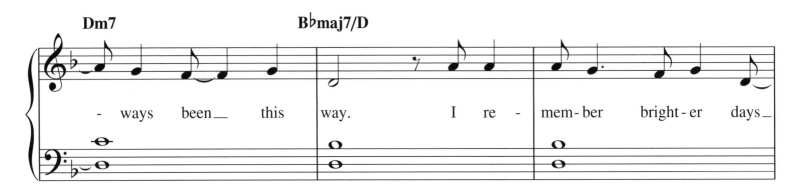

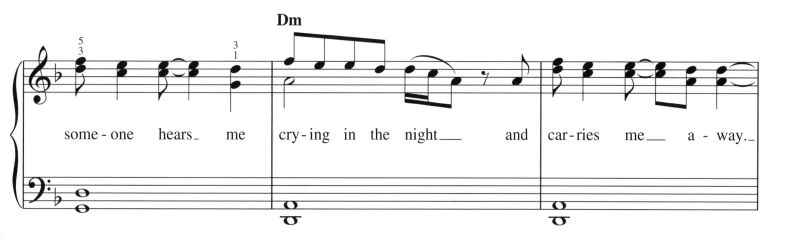

Set me free _____ of the

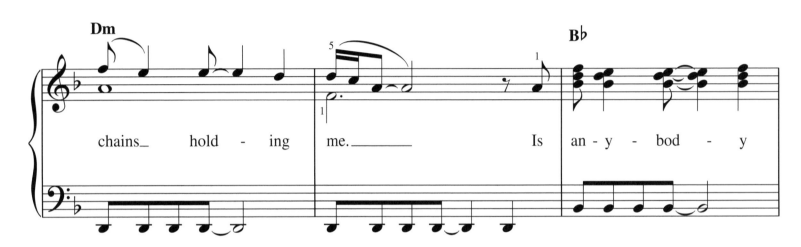

chains__ hold - ing me._____ Is an - y - bod - y

out there hear-ing me?_____ Set me

free.

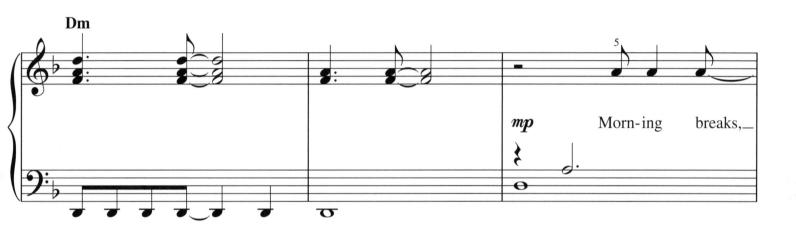

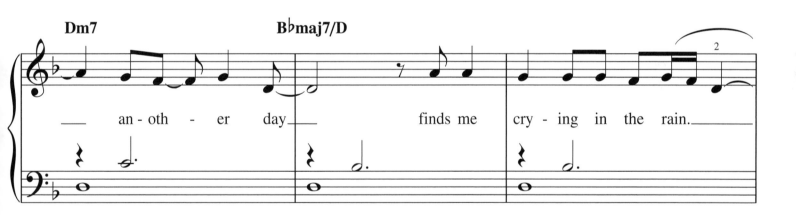

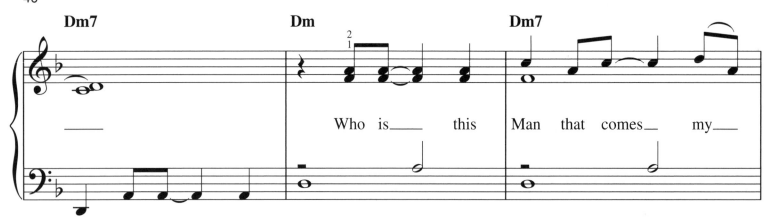

WHILE YOU WERE SLEEPING

Words and Music by
MARK HALL

Oh lit - tle town of Beth - le - hem, ___ looks like an - oth - er si - lent night. ___

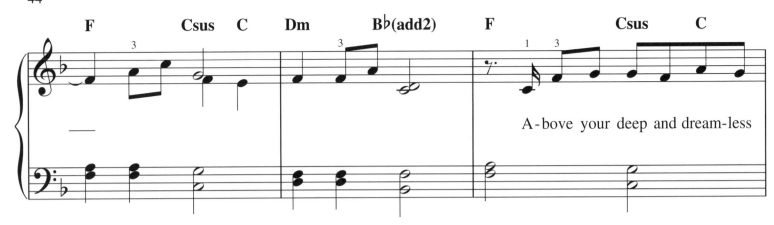

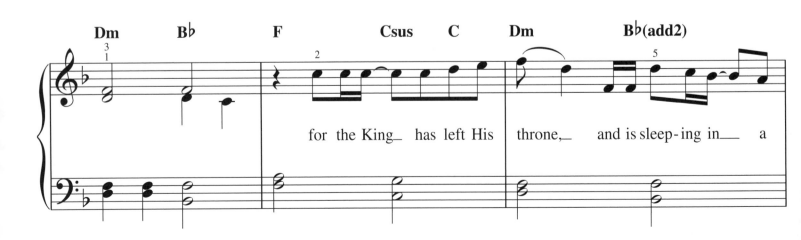

man-ger to - night,____ to - night.__ Oh Beth - le- hem, what you__ have
Je - ru - sa - lem, what you__ have

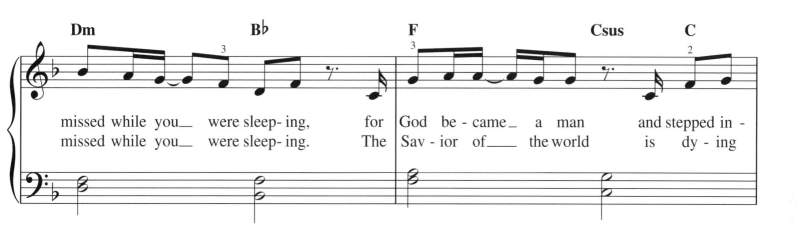

missed while you__ were sleep- ing, for God be - came_ a man and stepped in -
missed while you__ were sleep- ing. The Sav - ior of___ the world is dy - ing

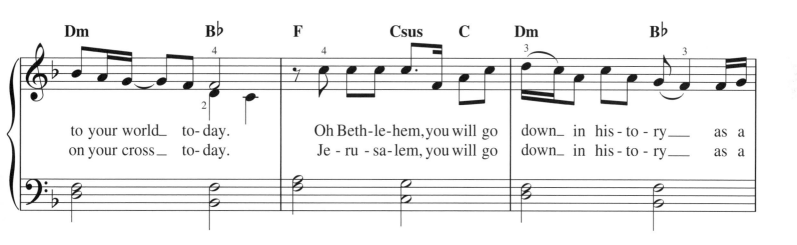

to your world__ to- day. Oh Beth-le-hem, you will go down_ in his - to - ry___ as a
on your cross__ to- day. Je - ru - sa-lem, you will go down_ in his - to - ry___ as a

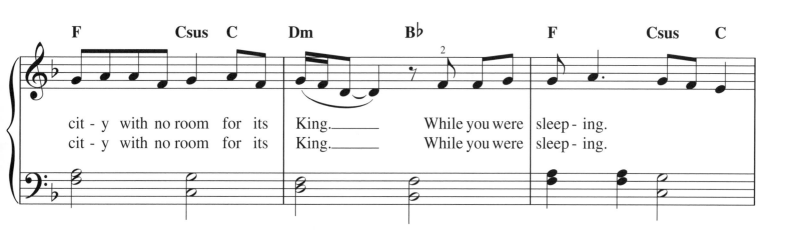

cit - y with no room for its King.____ While you were sleep - ing.
cit - y with no room for its King.____ While you were sleep - ing.

While you were sleep-ing.
While you were sleep-ing.

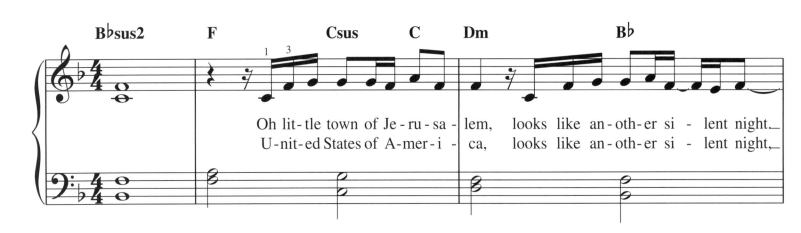

Oh lit-tle town of Je-ru-sa-lem, looks like an-oth-er si - lent night.___
U-nit-ed States of A-mer-i-ca, looks like an-oth-er si - lent night,___

___ The Fa-ther gave_ His on-ly Son; the
___

Way, the Truth,_ the Life had come. But there was no room_ for Him in the

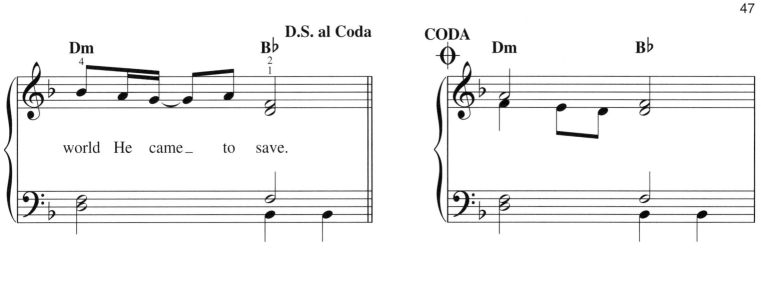

D.S. al Coda   **CODA**

world He came to save.

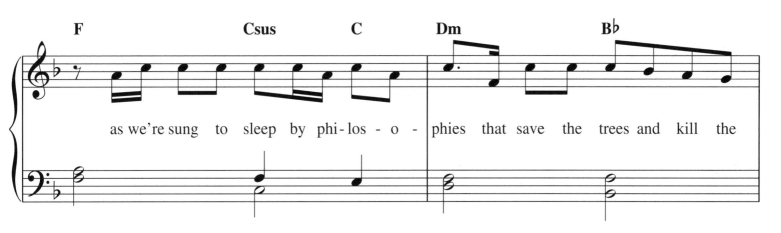

as we're sung to sleep by phi-los-o-phies that save the trees and kill the

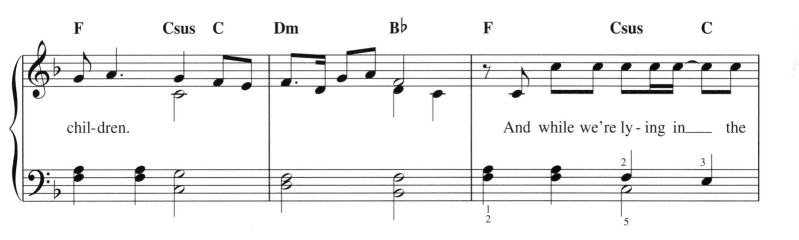

chil-dren.   And while we're ly-ing in____ the

dark,   there's a shout heard 'cross the east-ern sky,____

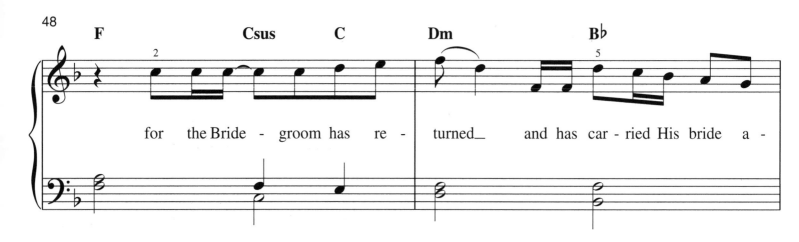

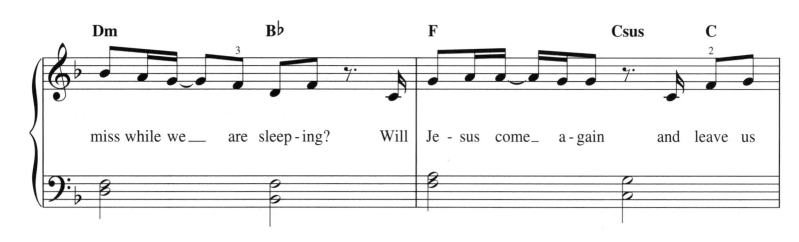

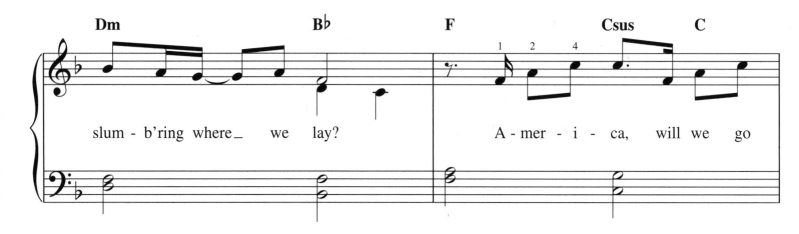

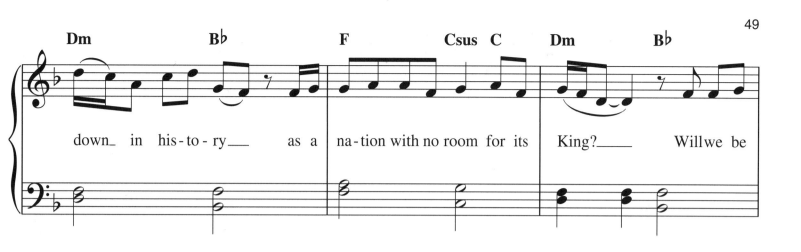

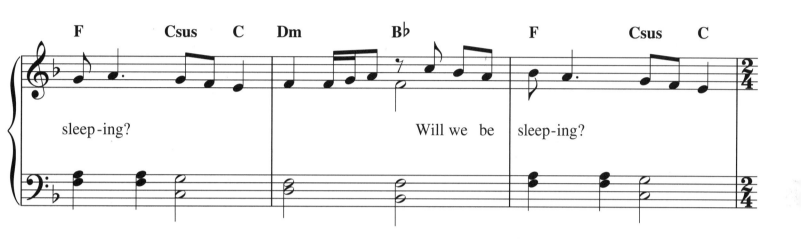

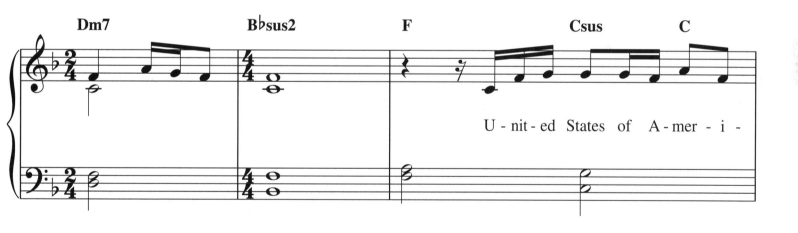

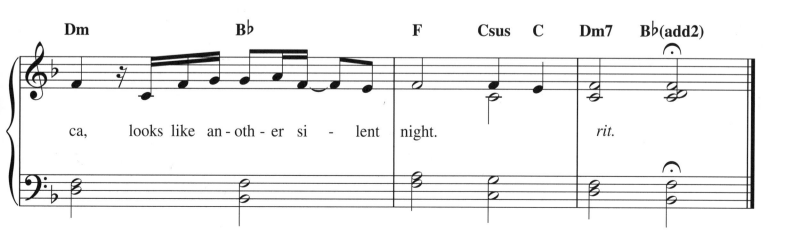

FATHER, SPIRIT, JESUS

Words and Music by MARK HALL,
CHAD CATES and DAVID HUNT

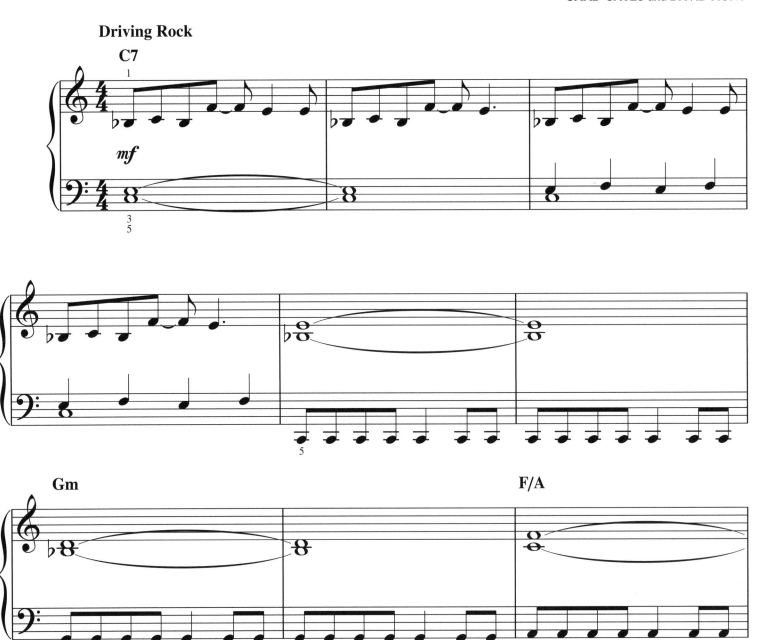

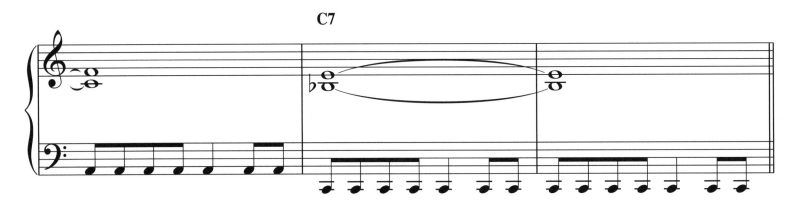

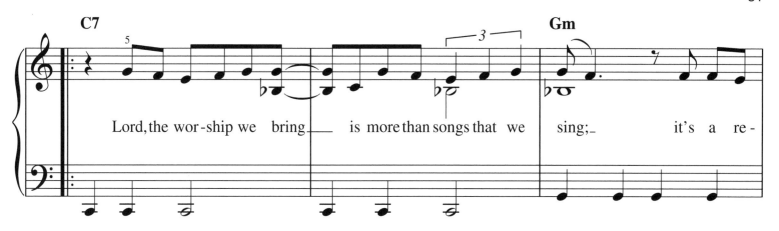

Lord, the wor-ship we bring___ is more than songs that we sing;___ it's a re-

flec - tion of our ev - er - chang - ing { lives,_____ / hearts,_____ } the

best we have___ to of - fer.

We don't just lift up our hands,___ Lord, we lift up our lives, ____ for we

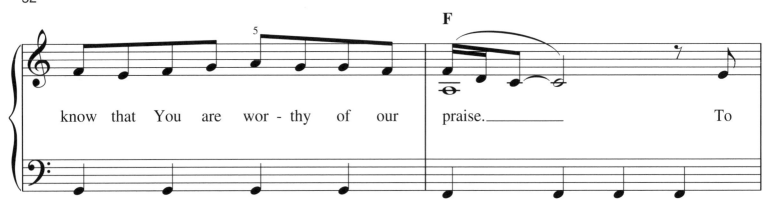

know that You are wor-thy of our praise._____ To

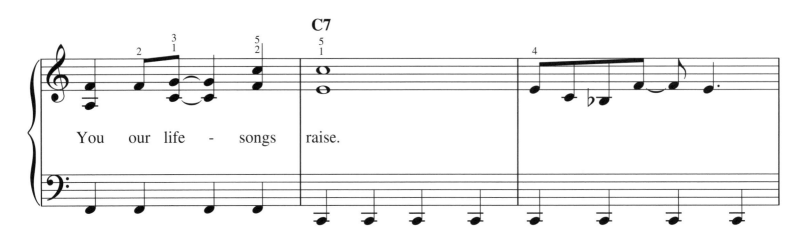

You our life - songs raise.

Res - cued from dark - ness,__ we are walk-ing in mar-vel-ous

light,_____ for we are chil-dren of___ the King!

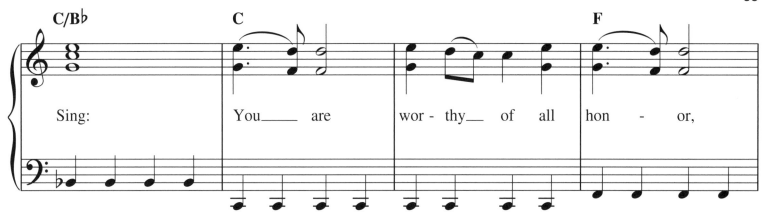

Sing: You__ are wor - thy__ of all hon - or,

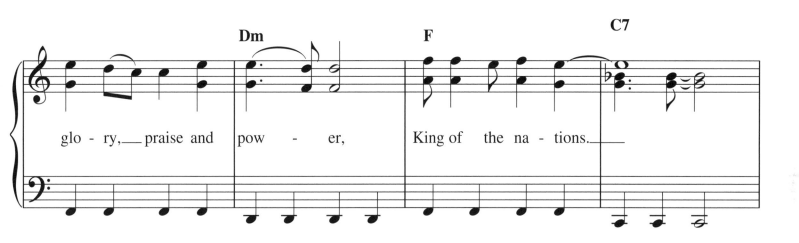

glo - ry,__ praise and pow — er, King of the na - tions.__

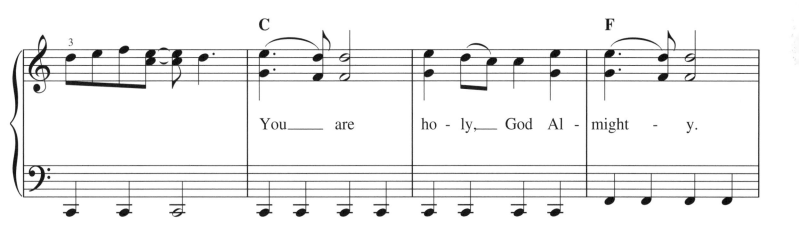

You__ are ho - ly,__ God Al - might - y.

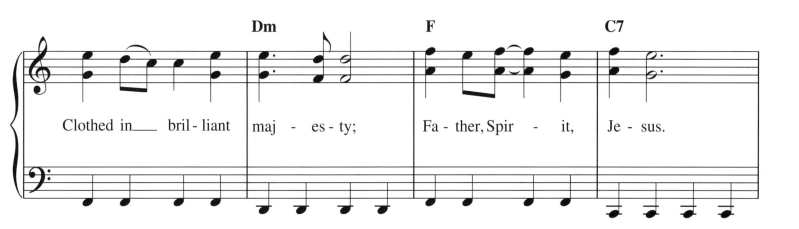

Clothed in__ bril - liant maj - es - ty; Fa - ther, Spir - it, Je - sus.

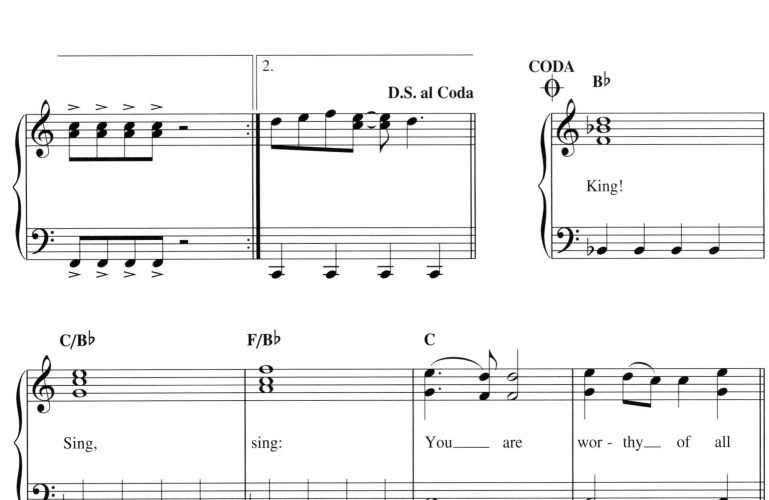

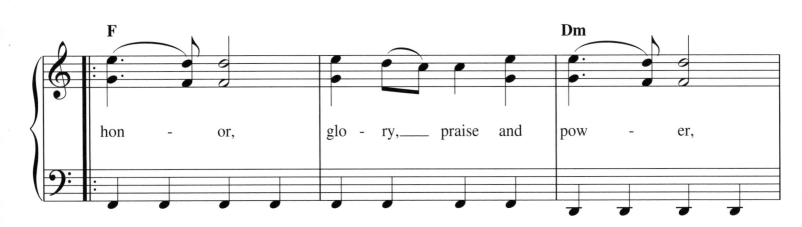

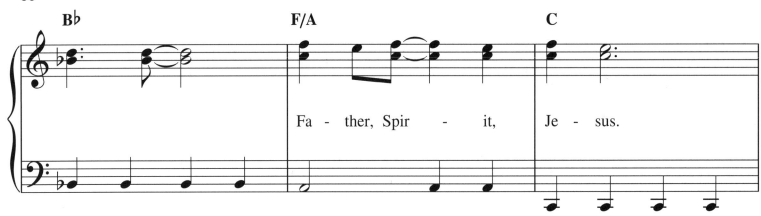

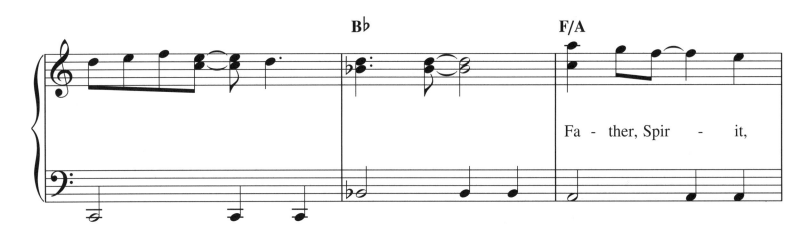

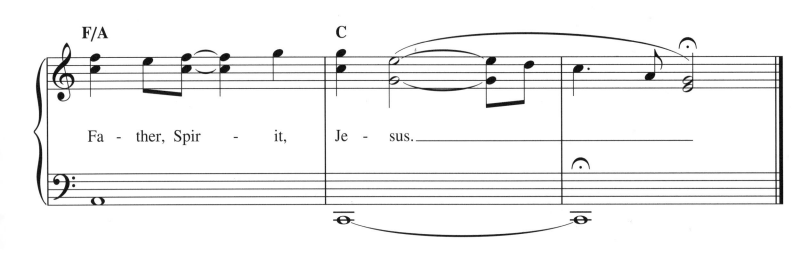

IN ME

Words and Music by
MARK HALL

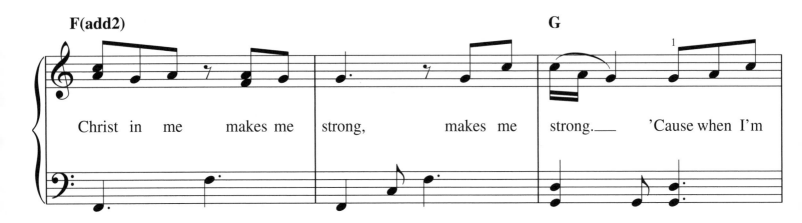

weak, You make me strong. When I'm blind, You shine___ Your

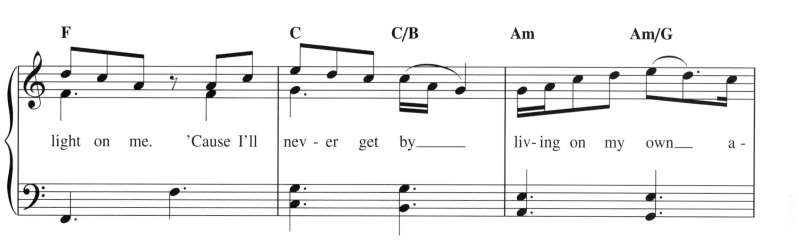

light on me. 'Cause I'll nev - er get by_____ liv-ing on my own___ a-

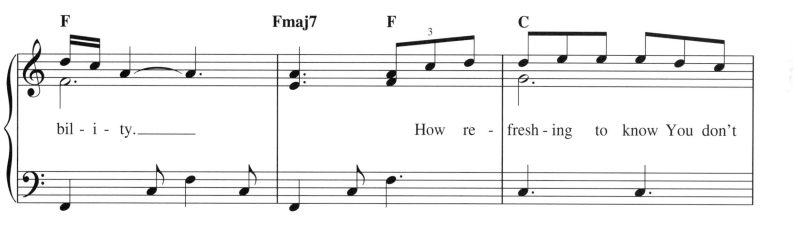

bil - i - ty._____ How re - fresh - ing to know You don't

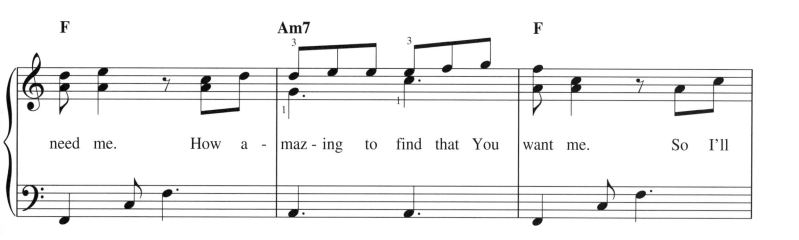

need me. How a - maz - ing to find that You want me. So I'll

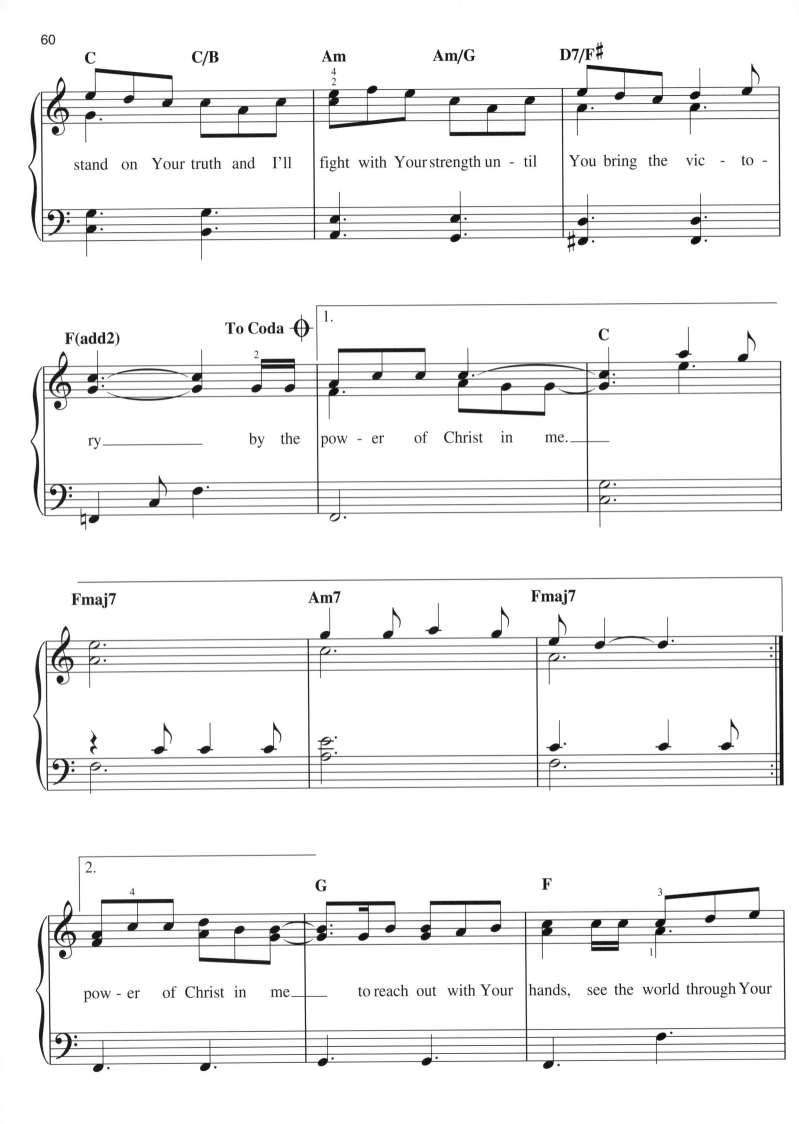

C **C/B** **Am** **Am/G** **D7/F#**

stand on Your truth and I'll fight with Your strength un - til You bring the vic - to -

F(add2) **To Coda ⊕** 1. **C**

ry_____ by the pow - er of Christ in me._____

Fmaj7 **Am7** **Fmaj7**

2. **G** **F**

pow - er of Christ in me____ to reach out with Your hands, see the world through Your

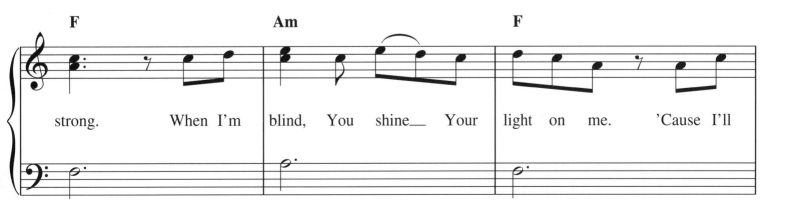

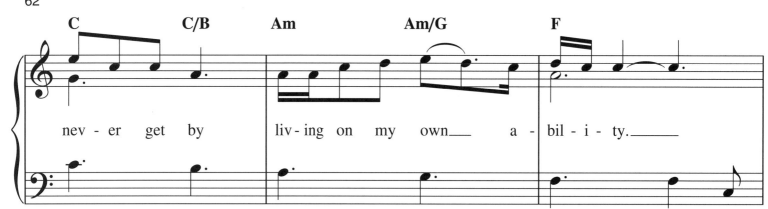

nev - er get by   liv - ing on my own___ a - bil - i - ty.___

D.S. al Coda

When I'm

CODA

pow - er of Christ in me,___   the

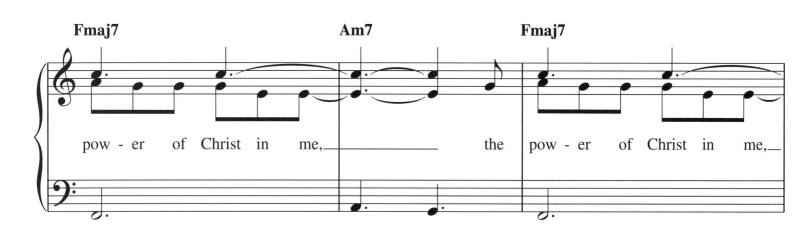

pow - er of Christ in me,   pow - er of Christ in me,___   the   pow - er of Christ in me,___

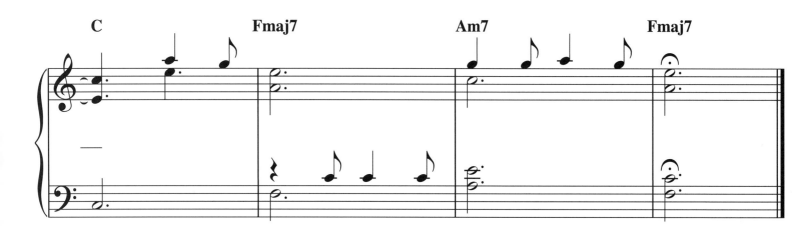

PRODIGAL

Words and Music by
MARK HALL

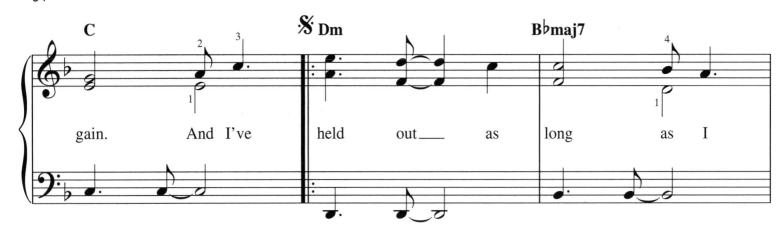

gain. And I've held out___ as long as I

can. Now I'm let - ting go___ and

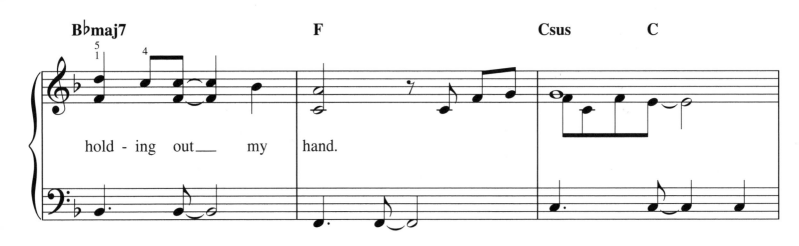

hold - ing out__ my hand.

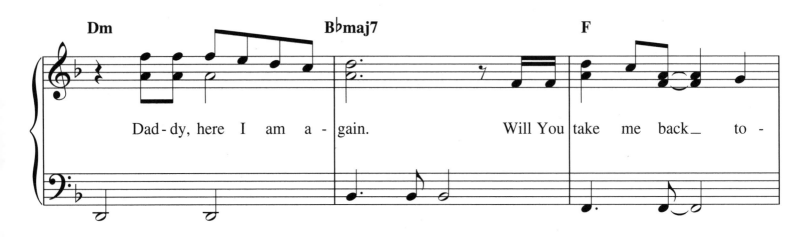

Dad - dy, here I am a - gain. Will You take me back_ to -

night? I went and made the world my friend, and it

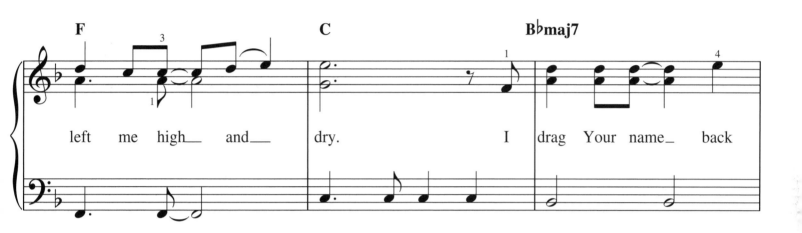

left me high and dry. I drag Your name back

through the mud that You first found me in. Not

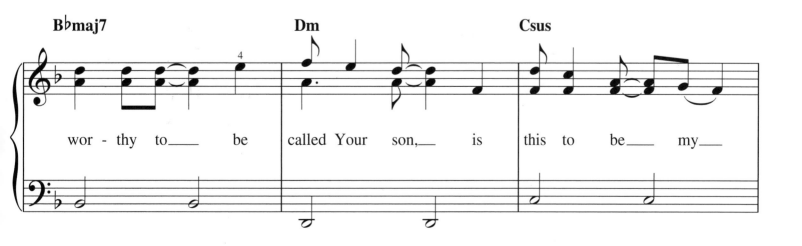

wor-thy to be called Your son, is this to be my

end?

Dad - dy, here I am,

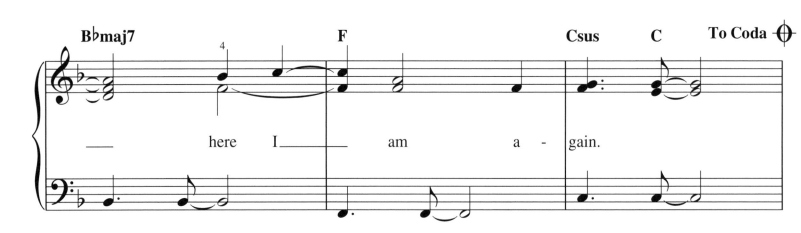

__ here I__ am a - gain.

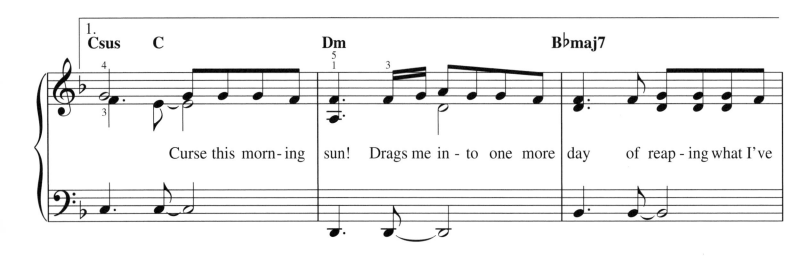

Curse this morn-ing sun! Drags me in-to one more day of reap-ing what I've

sown,   of liv - ing with my | shame.   Wel-come to my | world   and the life that I have

made,   where one day you're a | prince,   the next day you're a | slave.   And I've

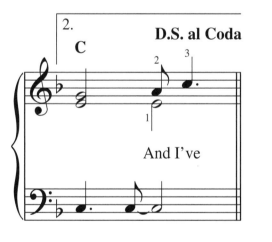

2.

D.S. al Coda

And I've

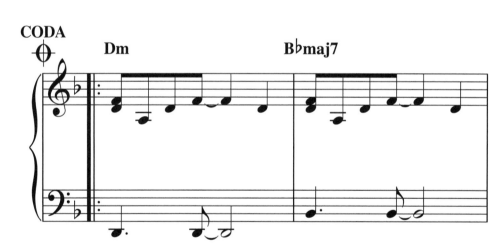

CODA

AND NOW MY LIFESONG SINGS

Words and Music by
MARK HALL

I once was lost, but now I'm found. I once was
blind, but now I see.

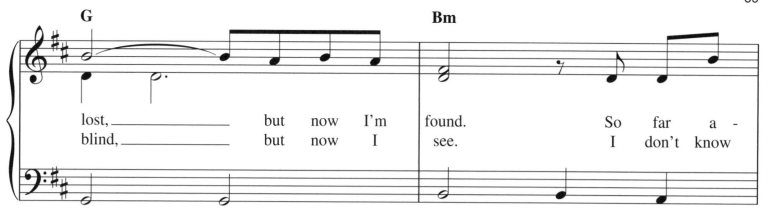

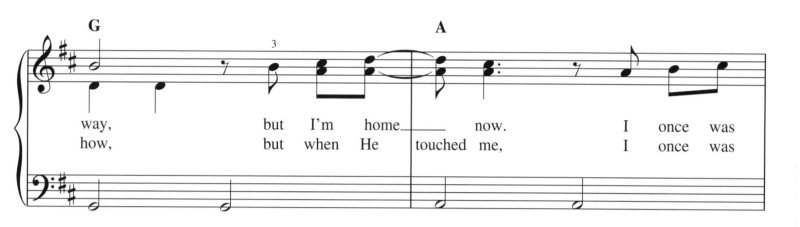

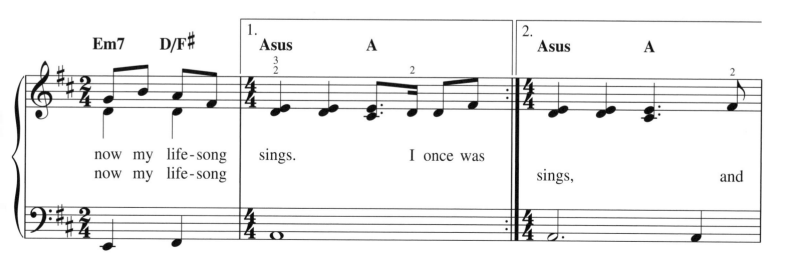

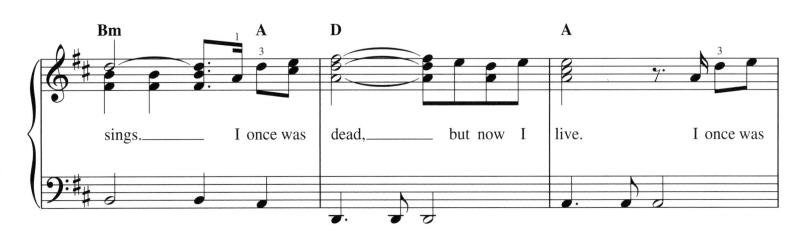

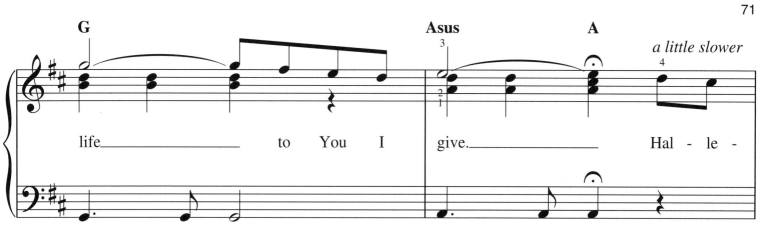

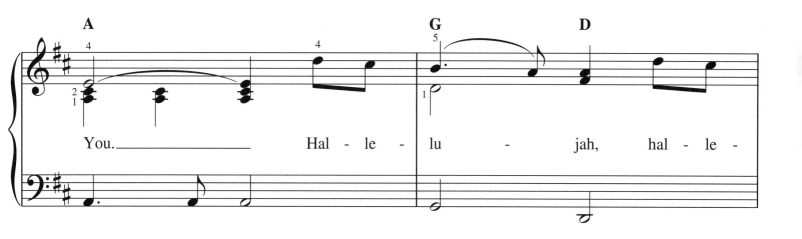

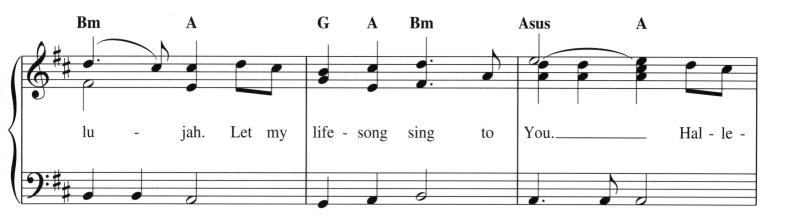

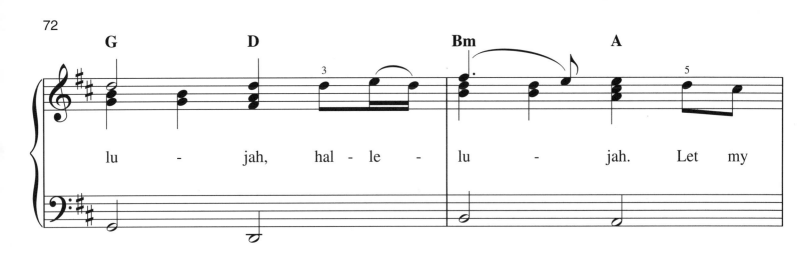

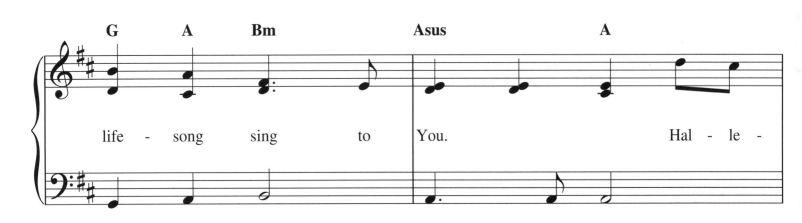

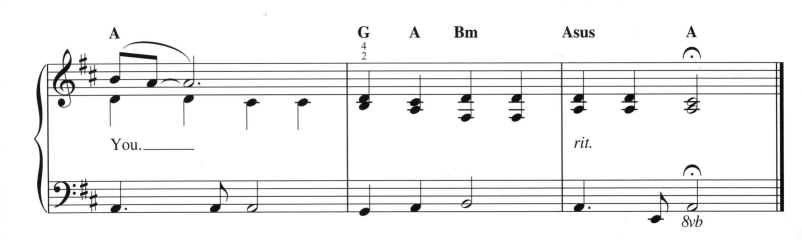